LV

13x $^{12}\!/_{05}$ (5/05)

17x 3/08-9/09

20x $\frac{2-12}{3-13}$

Harriet Tubman

A Photo-Illustrated Biography
by Margo McLoone

Reading Consultant:
Dr. Gail Lowe
Anacostia Museum

Bridgestone Books
an Imprint of Capstone Press

Facts about Harriet Tubman

- Harriet Tubman made at least 15 trips to free slaves.
- A total of $40,000 cash was offered for her capture.
- She served as a spy and a nurse in the Civil War.
- Her face is on a U.S. postage stamp.

Bridgestone Books are published by Capstone Press
151 Good Counsel Drive, P.O. Box 669, Mankato, Minnesota 56002
http://www.capstone-press.com

Library of Congress Cataloging-in-Publication Data
McLoone, Margo.
    Harriet Tubman/by Margo McLoone.
    p. cm.--(Read and discover photo-illustrated biographies)
    Includes bibliographical references and index.
    Summary: A brief biography of the woman who escaped life as a slave and then rescued
    hundreds of other slaves as a conductor in the underground railroad.
    ISBN 1-56065-519-4
1. Tubman, Harriet, 1820?-1913--Juvenile literature. 2. Slaves--United States--Biography--
Juvenile literature. 3. Afro-Americans--Biography--Juvenile literature. 4. Afro-American
women--Biography--Juvenile literature. 5. Underground railroad--Juvenile literature.
[1. Tubman, Harriet, 1820?-1913. 2. Slaves. 3. Afro-Americans--Biography. 4. Women--
Biography. 5. Underground railroad.]
I. Title. II. Series.
E444.T82M377   1997
305.5'67'092
[B]--DC21

                                                    96-37383
                                                       CIP
                                                        AC

Photo credits
Schomburg Center, cover, 16, 18, 20
Unicorn/Aneal F. Vohra, 4; Bunde, 6, 8
Bettmann, 10, 12, 14

    4 5 6 04 03 02

Table of Contents

4

Brave Conductor

Harriet Tubman helped hundreds of African Americans escape from slavery. A slave is a person who is owned by someone else. Harriet was a slave. She escaped to freedom and then helped others escape.

Harriet worked to stop slavery. She became part of the Underground Railroad. The Underground Railroad was a group of safe houses. Slaves who ran away traveled from house to house. Each home owner helped slaves escape to freedom in the north. Slavery was against the law in the northern United States.

The brave people who led the slaves north were known as conductors. Harriet was a famous conductor.

Harriet was a slave who escaped to freedom.

Young Slave

Harriet Tubman was born in 1821 in Dorchester County, Maryland. She was one of 11 children in her family. Her parents were Harriet and Benjamin Ross. She was named Araminta, but her family called her Minty. When she was 13, she was given her adult name. Her adult name was Harriet.

Harriet started working when she was six years old. She worked in her owner's house. She dusted tables and scrubbed floors. She cared for a baby.

Harriet's owner was not kind to her. Harriet was often beaten. She slept on cold floors. She had very little food to eat.

When she was seven years old, Harriet tried to run away. After escaping, she became hungry and tired. She returned to her owner.

Harriet's family might have lived in a house like this one.

Escape Attempt

Harriet was not a good housekeeper. She was sent to work in the fields. The work was harder. But Harriet liked being outside.

One day, Harriet was picking cotton in a field. She saw a slave leave the field. She followed him to a nearby store.

The owner caught up with them. He told Harriet to help him catch the other slave. She refused. The owner threw a heavy weight at her head. It hit her forehead. She fell to the ground, nearly dead.

Harriet never fully healed. She had a deep scar. Throughout her life, she suffered from headaches and fainting spells.

Harriet was not a good housekeeper. She picked cotton in the fields.

Escape to Freedom

In 1844, Harriet married John Tubman. He had been a slave. But now he was free because his master had died. Harriet wanted her freedom, too. She knew African Americans were free in the North.

Harriet asked John to escape to the North with her. He said no. Harriet did not lose her dream. She said she would go free or die.

One night, Harriet left home in secret. She went to a trusted woman's house. The woman gave her directions to her next stop. Harriet would be safe at these places.

Harriet was hidden in a wagon and driven far away. Then she continued her journey. In 1849, she made it safely to the North. She was free.

Harriet stayed at several safe places. They were similar to this Underground Railroad stop near Albany, Kansas.

Return

Harriet worked as a hotel maid in Philadelphia, Pennsylvania. She missed her family. She made plans to help them escape, too.

On Christmas Eve in 1850, Harriet returned to Maryland. She came for her three brothers and their families.

It was not safe to tell their parents the plan. Harriet's father, Ben, covered his eyes. He wanted to tell his owner that he did not see anything.

Harriet safely led her brothers and their families north. She later returned for her most daring trip. She took her aging parents north to freedom.

Harriet helped lead both her family and other slaves to freedom.

Bold Rescuer

From 1850 to 1861, Harriet made at least 15 trips to free slaves. It was very dangerous. By law, slaves who ran away to the North could be captured. Then, they were returned to their owners.

Slaves were not safe anywhere in the United States. People put up posters offering a reward for Harriet's capture. She started to lead slaves farther north to Canada.

Harriet hid herself in many ways. She moved through swamp water and rivers. This kept bloodhounds from finding her scent. The dogs could not track her. Harriet also carried a pistol for security.

Harriet led more than 300 slaves to freedom. She never lost one person. She was never caught. Her final trip was in late 1860.

Posters offered a reward for Harriet's capture.

Civil War Spy

In 1861, the Civil War began. A civil war is a conflict between people within the same country. Harriet joined soldiers fighting for the North. She fought against slavery in the South. She served as a nurse for wounded soldiers. She went into enemy territory to spy on troops.

Once, Harriet went on a rescue mission with northern troops. They freed more than 750 slaves from prisons. Harriet served in the army for three years. People called her General Tubman.

In 1863, President Abraham Lincoln issued the Emancipation Proclamation. This written order freed all slaves in the United States. The war ended two years later. The northern states won.

Harriet served as a nurse, a spy, and a soldier in the Civil War.

Last Years

After the Civil War, Harriet brought her parents to New York. They lived in her house.

Harriet was free but poor. The army promised to pay her. Eventually she received payments of 20 dollars a month.

In 1869, Sarah Bradford wrote a book about Harriet. It was called *Scenes in the Life of Harriet Tubman*. Harriet earned money from the book's sales.

In 1869, Harriet married Nelson Davis. He was a Civil War soldier.

In 1908, Harriet opened a home in Auburn, New York. The home was for older African Americans. Harriet was 75 years old herself. But she continued to care for others.

Harriet brought her aging parents to her home in New York.

Daring Woman

Harriet risked her life to help other people. She was not afraid of danger.

Harriet continued her work after slavery ended. She fought for the rights of freed slaves. She worked to give women the right to vote. She built a home for poor and older African Americans. It was called the Harriet Tubman Home.

Harriet Tubman died in Auburn, New York, in 1913. She was nearly 93 years old. Today tourists still visit her home.

Harriet lived to be nearly 93 years old.

Words from Harriet Tubman

"I had reasoned this out in my mind; there was one of two things I had a right to, liberty or death; if I could not have one, I would have the other; for no man should take me alive."

From the book about Harriet Tubman's life, *Scenes in the Life of Harriet Tubman,* published in 1869.

"On my underground railroad I never ran my train off the track and I never lost a passenger. "

From the book about Harriet Tubman's life, *Scenes in the Life of Harriet Tubman,* published in 1869.

Important Dates in Harriet Tubman's Life

1821—Born a slave in Dorchester County, Maryland

1833—Injured by a blow to the head

1844—Marries John Tubman

1849—Escapes from slavery to Philadelphia, Pennsylvania

1850—Makes the first trip south to rescue slaves

1857—Rescues her parents from slavery

1861—Works as a nurse for the Northern army in the Civil War

1863—Serves as a spy for the Northern army in the Civil War

1869—Sarah Bradford publishes Harriet's biography

1869—Marries Nelson Davis

1908—Builds a home for the sick and elderly in Auburn, New York

1913—Dies in Auburn, New York

Words to Know

civil war (SIV-il WOR)—a conflict between different groups of people within the same country.

conductor (kuhn-DUHK-tur)—a person who led runaway slaves north

Emancipation Proclamation (i-man-si-PAY-shun pruh-klah-MAY-shun)—a written order signed by President Abraham Lincoln that freed all slaves.

slave (SLAYV)—a person who is owned by someone else

Underground Railroad (UHN-dur-ground RAYL-rohd)—a group of safe houses.

Read More

Rau, Dana Meachen. *Harriet Tubman.* Compass Point Early Biographies. Minneapolis: Compass Point Books, 2001.

Schraff, Anne E. *Harriet Tubman: Moses of the Underground Railroad.* African-American Biographies. Berkeley Heights, NJ: Enslow, 2000.

Stein, R. Conrad. *The Underground Railroad.* Cornerstones of Freedom. New York: Children's Press, 1997.

Useful Addresses and Internet Sites

Anacostia Museum
1901 Fort Place, South East
Washington, DC 20020

The Harriet Tubman Home
180 South Street
Auburn, NY 13021

Black History Month—Biography—Harriet Tubman
http://www.galegroup.com/free_resources/bhm/bio/tubman_h.htm
Harriet Tubman & The Underground Railroad
http://www2.lhric.org/pocantico/tubman/tubman.html

Index